THE POWER OF NETWORKING

Achieving Success through Navigation

BY

Maxen Faisal

Copyright © 2023 by Maxen Faisal

TABLE OF CONTENTS

INTRODUCTION

In a connected world, networking is a strong force that has the potential to significantly impact both our personal and professional lives.

A crucial component of success is now the capacity to create and maintain relationships, look for opportunities, and absorb knowledge from the experiences of others. Welcome to "The Power of Networking," an exploration of this transformative force that has the power to help you achieve your goals and aspirations.

Networking goes beyond the limitations of conventional career advancement and is frequently regarded as both an art and a science. It is the art of establishing deep bonds and forming partnerships that may lead to opportunities you were unaware of. It is the science of comprehending the human dynamics underlying these connections and of appreciating the psychology that underlies every successful interaction.

The principles of networking apply to everyone, whether you're an aspiring professional, an established business owner, or just someone who wants to broaden their horizons.

Through the various aspects of networking—from mastering the art of conversation to utilizing the limitless potential of digital platforms—we will help you navigate the complexities of networking in this book.

We'll look at the methods and approaches that can support you in creating relationships that last and benefit both parties in your personal and professional lives.

However, networking is more than just exchanging business cards and adding LinkedIn connections.

It's about the shared journey toward development and success, the sharing of ideas, and the building of trust in the context of the human experience.

Finding partners who can complement your strengths, mentors who can illuminate your path, and a community that can offer support during trying times are all important.

You'll read about people who have accomplished amazing things by using networking throughout this book.

Their experiences are proof of the networking's capacity for transformation, from professional successes to business successes.

We'll also delve into the nuances of networking for personal development, education, and promoting your wellbeing. Because networking transcends the boardroom and affects every aspect of our lives, enabling us to grow and become better versions of ourselves.

This book will provide insights catered to your specific personality and objectives, whether you're an extrovert looking to improve your approach or an introvert looking to navigate networking events with confidence.
Regardless of temperament or experience level, networking is for everyone.

I urge you to approach this exploration of the power of networking with an open mind and a curious heart as we begin. Be ready to push yourself beyond your comfort zone, embrace the art of connection, and open doors you never imagined were possible.

Your journey has begun.

Let's use networking to its fullest potential.

CHAPTER 1

THE ESSENCE OF NETWORKING

The Key to Success.

Networking is the thread that weaves connections, creates opportunities, and unlocks doors in the vast tapestry of human interaction. It is the foundation of both personal and professional development and the art of establishing relationships.
It is also the science of comprehending human dynamics.
We set out on a journey to explore the fundamentals of networking in this chapter, including its essence, the psychology behind effective networking, and how to set specific networking objectives that will direct your career.

1 Understanding What Networking Is All About.

Connection is the central concept of networking. It is a conscious effort made with the intention of fostering relationships with others for the benefit of both parties.
Recognizing networking's fundamental components is the first step in understanding it.

Building Bridges, Not Islands: Networking is about building bridges between individuals, organizations, and concepts.
It focuses on fostering collaboration and tearing down silos.

The Value of Trust: The foundation of all enduring relationships is trust.
Genuineness, openness, and respect for one another are also important components of trust.

Mutual Gain and Reciprocity: Networking successfully requires both parties to contribute. It entails sharing equally with those around you while also keeping in mind that ultimately, both parties must benefit.

2 The Psychology of Successful Networking.

Understanding the psychology behind each meaningful connection is essential for effective networking, which goes beyond cursory interactions. Investigate the psychology of successful networking as you start your networking journey, which includes:.

Active listening and empathetic listening go hand in hand, and they are the foundation of developing deep connections.
It entails truly comprehending the wants, needs, and difficulties of others.

Nonverbal communication and body language make up the majority of human interaction.
You can convey sincerity and build rapport by becoming adept at reading nonverbal cues and body language.

The Influence of First Impression: Initial impressions are important.
When meeting new people, learn how to leave a lasting impression.

3 Developing networking objectives.

Having definite objectives is crucial for successfully navigating the complex world of networking.
Without a plan, networking can result in pointless interactions.
You can: by setting networking goals.

Establish Your Objectives: Decide what you hope to accomplish through networking.
Is it personal development, learning, business growth, or career advancement?

Specify the kinds of people or organizations you want to connect with to achieve your goals when identifying key connections.

Establish Milestones: Divide your networking journey into manageable milestones to help you track progress and maintain motivation.

Keep in mind that these guiding principles are the cornerstone on which your networking success will be built as we delve deeper into the power of networking.
In addition to being a transactional activity, networking is a transformative journey that can result in remarkable personal and professional growth.

The practical methods and approaches that will translate these fundamentals into concrete outcomes will be covered in the upcoming chapters. Prepare to realize networking's full potential.

CHAPTER 2

MAKE YOUR NETWORKING TOOLKIT.

Making connections with skill and grace.

In order to be successful, networking requires a well-stocked toolkit and is not a passive activity. The key components of your networking toolkit are covered in this chapter, including how to create an effective elevator pitch, how to make small talk, and how to behave when meeting new people. Utilizing these resources will give you the confidence you need to move through networking situations and make an impression that will lead to opportunities.

1 Making Your Elevator Pitch,

Your introduction to networking is through your elevator pitch.
It's a succinct, powerful statement that conveys who you are, what you do, and the value you add.
In order to create a powerful elevator pitch, you must:.

Keep it concise and impactful while maintaining clarity. Your elevator pitch should be short enough to be delivered in that amount of time.

Putting Your Special Value in the Foreground:
Stress what makes you stand out. What qualities, experiences, or skills distinguish you as a valuable connection?

Engaging and Memorable: Your elevator pitch
ought to pique interest and be memorable.
To make your points more vivid, tell stories or give
anecdotes.

2 Developing Your Small Talk Skills.

The first connections made through networking are
held together by small talk, which serves as social
glue.
The ability to strike up casual conversations is what
helps people feel at ease and break the ice.
In order to master the art of small talk:.

Encourage conversation by posing open-ended questions that elicit more information than a simple "yes" or "no" response.

Actively listening means being aware of what the other person is saying and demonstrating a sincere interest in their responses.

To promote a sense of connection, look for areas of commonality by identifying shared experiences, goals, or interests.

3 The Dos and Don'ts of Networking Etiquette.

Effective networking involves more than just what you say; it also involves your behavior.
Following appropriate networking etiquette can mean the difference between a successful interaction and a lost opportunity.
Key dos and don'ts are listed below:.

Do:.

When attending networking events, arrive on time.

Immediately follow up with new contacts.

When someone helps you or gives you advice, thank them for it.

Don't:.

disrupt or take over conversations.

Don't divulge personal information too much.

to pursue opportunities with an excessive amount of vigor or pushiness.

Building your networking toolkit requires constant practice, improvement, and adaptability.
Keep in mind that networking isn't just about what you can get out of it; it's also about what you can give to others as you develop these skills and strategies.
We'll delve into the complexities of networking in various contexts and examine more sophisticated techniques in the upcoming chapters. Prepare to transform your networking encounters into meaningful connections that can reshape your future.

CHAPTER 3

INTERNET NETWORKING IN THE DIGITAL AGE.

Creating Connections Across Boundaries.

The digital age has completely changed the way we communicate, creating a plethora of brand-new opportunities for networking and establishing connections.
We'll examine the dynamics of networking in the digital sphere in this chapter.

We'll talk about how to use social media effectively, use LinkedIn to network professionally, and participate in online forums and communities.
With the help of these resources, you'll be able to broaden your network, forge lasting relationships, and acclimate to the changing networking environment of the twenty-first century.

1 Using social media to network.

Social media platforms have developed into virtual hubs for networking, providing chances to get in touch with a large audience.
In order to effectively use social media for networking:.

Select the social media channels that are most compatible with your networking objectives.
Every social media platform, including Facebook, Instagram, and Twitter, has its own advantages.

Share Value: To position yourself as a thought leader in your sector, contribute insightful content, knowledge, and experience.

Actively participate in your network by joining groups that are relevant to you, responding to discussions, and leaving comments.

2 The Influence of Professional Networking and LinkedIn.

The professional networking site LinkedIn has a lot of potential for developing a powerful network.

Utilize LinkedIn's potential by doing the following.

Optimize Your Profile: Create a compelling LinkedIn profile that focuses on your abilities, successes, and experiences.

Connect Strategically: Establish a network of contacts, including those with colleagues, mentors, and peers in your industry, that supports your professional objectives.

Share Thoughtful Content: To interact with your network and show your knowledge, share articles, updates, and insights from the industry.

3 Online forums and communities.

Online forums and communities offer niches where people with similar interests can connect. Making connections and learning from these communities can come from participation. Effectively navigating online communities requires that.

Determine Relevance: Look for groups or discussion forums that share your interests, passions, or goals for your career.

Think Before You Post: Participate actively by posing queries, sharing your knowledge, and abiding by community rules.

Create Connections: Talk to other members who have similar interests and objectives to your own, and think about taking these connections offline.

The opportunities for connection and collaboration provided by networking in the digital age are unmatched.
The digital environment can be a strong ally if you're looking to grow your professional network, make connections with like-minded people, or keep up with market trends.
Further methods for growing your network both online and offline will be covered in the chapters that follow. Prepare to use the digital tools at your disposal and to take advantage of networking opportunities in our connected world.

CHAPTER 4

CULTIVATING MEANINGFUL CONNECTIONS

The Heart of Networking

Networking is about forming lasting, beneficial relationships, not just amassing contacts.

This chapter explores the fundamental principles of creating genuine connections, highlighting the significance of being authentic, fostering relationships for lasting achievements, and establishing trust and credibility.

These principles are the foundation for enduring, mutually advantageous networking connections.

The Significance of Authenticity in Networking

Unlock your networking potential with authenticity. Authenticity requires honesty, openness, and being true to oneself.
Here\\\'s why authenticity matters:

Genuine authenticity builds trust by fostering connection and gaining people's trust.

Authenticity brings like-minded connections, forming meaningful relationships.

Authentic relationships last due to honesty and mutual respect.

Cultivating Relationships for Sustained Success

Networking requires continual relationship building, not just one-time interactions.
To cultivate lasting relationships for success.

Maintain connection: Periodically message, email, or call to stay in touch with your network.

Contribute to your network's success by offering value through assistance, insights, or support.

Recognize and rejoice in the accomplishments and milestones of those you are connected to, to enhance your bond with them.

Establishing Confidence And Trustworthiness.

Networking requires trust.
It's the basis for building productive connections.
To gain trust and build credibility:

Maintain consistency: Be consistent and reliable in
your actions and commitments.
Consistent actions build trust over time.

Keep your promises: Fulfill your commitments.
This establishes a dependable reputation.

Share your expertise generously, positioning
yourself as a valuable resource for knowledge.

Nurturing meaningful connections demands
patience, sincerity, and effort.
Your present relationships can unexpectedly and
profoundly influence your future.
Your authenticity, nurturing, trust, and credibility
will distinguish you in networking.
Get ready to enhance connections and maximize
network potential.

CHAPTER 5

STRATEGIES TO NETWORK FOR INTROVERTS AND EXTROVERTS

Discovering Your Personality's Power

Networking benefits introverts and extroverts, who leverage their individual strengths.
This chapter examines customized networking tactics for both types of personalities.
We'll cover networking strategies for introverts, maximizing opportunities for extroverts, and universal principles for networking success, no matter your personality.

You can confidently navigate the networking world by embracing and utilizing your inherent qualities.

Effective Networking Strategies for Introverts

Introverts' active listening, empathy, and thoughtfulness give them advantages in networking. Succeed in networking as an introvert:

Plan and Practice: Prior to networking events, plan key points and practice your elevator pitch to boost confidence.

Prioritize Quality over Quantity: Strive for meaningful connections with a select few rather than superficial connections with many.

Engage in active listening to show genuine interest in others during meaningful conversations.

Maximizing Networking Opportunities for Outgoing Individuals

Socially skilled extroverts excel in networking.
As an extrovert, maximize networking opportunities.

Start conversations confidently and approach new people with enthusiasm.

Connect widely and leverage your network by utilizing your social skills.

Maintain a balance between talking and listening:
Actively listen and engage in two-way conversations
for meaningful connections.

.3 Achieving Networking Success, No Matter Your Personality

All personality types can achieve networking
success.
Networking success is influenced by universal
principles, regardless of your disposition.

Stay genuine: Embrace your true self and
communicate authentically.
Authenticity resonates with others.

Establishing specific objectives: Clearly outline
desired outcomes and goals for every networking
interaction.

Networking success often depends on follow-up and
nurturing.
Maintain communication with your contacts and
cultivate relationships over the long term.

Networking accommodates the strengths of both
introverts and extroverts.
Maximize your strengths through personalized
approaches for networking success.
In the upcoming chapters, we'll delve into more
tactics and scenarios to boost your networking skills
and abilities.
Unlock your networking potential, regardless of
your personality type.

CHAPTER 6

PROFESSIONAL NETWORKING IN AREA.

Building Strategic Connections.

Connecting with like-minded people, subject matter experts, and potential partners can be accomplished through networking in professional settings. In this chapter, we'll explore the nuances of networking in business settings, including techniques for meeting people at seminars and conferences, how to network successfully at trade shows, and the significant benefits of developing your personal brand through networking.

You can improve your professional network and broaden your horizons by strategically navigating these environments.

1 Networking at seminars and conferences.

A wealth of information and networking opportunities can be found at conferences and seminars. To get the most out of these occasions, do the following.

Research speakers, attendees, and topics in advance to find potential connections and conversation starters.

Engage Actively: Participate in discussions, attend sessions, and ask questions to show that you are knowledgeable and interested.

Connect with people you meet on professional networking sites like LinkedIn and send them personalized follow-up messages after the event.

2 Successful Networking at Business Events.

Trade shows, product launches, and industry mixers are all excellent places to network in the business world. To successfully navigate these events, do the following.

Establish Specific Goals: Outline your objectives for the event, including any connections you want to make, market research you want to do, or possible collaborations you want to find.

Create a memorable elevator pitch and practice making confident introductions to master the art of introduction.

Prioritize the quality of your connections over the quantity of your business cards by concentrating on making a select number of deep connections.

3. Using networking to develop your personal brand.

Building your personal brand can be accomplished through networking. Your professional image and reputation are what make up your personal brand. What networking can do for your personal brand is listed below.

Messaging Consistency: To strengthen your brand identity, consistently communicate your special value proposition to your network.

To establish yourself as a thought leader, share your knowledge and insights in articles, talks, or other forums.

Leveraging Your Network: Work together with your network to strengthen your individual brand and assist your professional endeavors.

Professional networking goes beyond socializing; it's a chance to establish yourself as a thought leader in your field, create lasting relationships, and advance your career.
We'll examine sophisticated networking success strategies in upcoming chapters in a variety of situations.
Get ready to hone your abilities and make an impression that will last in formal settings.

CHAPTER 7

ADVANCEMENT IN CAREER THROUGH NETWORKING.

Providing Fuel for Your Professional Journey.

Making connections is only one aspect of networking; it can also advance your career.
We explore networking tactics designed to advance careers in this chapter.
We'll look at how to use your network to your advantage to find employment, how to use

networking to advance professionally, and how to use networking to your advantage when switching careers or starting your own business.
You can advance your professional career to new heights by becoming an expert in these networking strategies.

1 Taking Advantage of Job Opportunities in Your Network.

When looking for employment opportunities, your network can be a helpful source. To effectively use your network, do the following.

Leverage Your Connections: Get in touch with people in your network who might be aware of job openings or who can introduce you to potential employers.

Create an effective job search strategy by utilizing your network to gather information about businesses and industries that interest you.
Then, adjust your job search as necessary.

Prepare for interviews by asking for advice and conducting mock interviews with network contacts who can offer insightful feedback.

2 Using Networking To Move Up The Corporate Ladder.

A strong tool for moving up within your current organization is networking.
utilizing networking, ascent up the corporate ladder.

Establish Connections Across Hierarchies: Make contact with coworkers, managers, and senior executives to increase exposure and visibility.

Find Mentors: Look for mentors in your company who can help you advance your career and offer insightful advice.

Participate in cross-functional projects to expand your network and skill set.
Work with colleagues from various departments.

3 Using Networking To Support Career Changes And Entrepreneurship.

Whether you're switching industries or starting your own business, networking can be a catalyst for career changes.
Here are some tips for effective networking.

Highlight experiences and skills from your current job that are useful in the field you want to enter by identifying your transferable skills.

Attend industry-specific events and network with professionals to establish connections with those who can offer advice and opportunities.

Establish a Supportive Network: Surround yourself with mentors, advisors, and other businesspeople who can provide guidance and advice.

The dynamic force of networking can help you find unanticipated opportunities and advance in your career.
We'll examine sophisticated networking techniques and delve into real-world situations in the upcoming chapters to further develop your networking skills.
Prepare to strategically network in order to advance your career.

CHAPTER 8

BUSINESS GROWTH THROUGH NETWORKING.

Providing Energy for Your Business Projects.

In addition to being a tool for professional development, networking is a significant factor in business expansion.
We'll look at networking tactics designed to help businesses expand in this chapter.

We'll go into detail about how to network successfully for small businesses, how to increase your clientele through networking, and how to network effectively with others to create fruitful business alliances.
You can help your business ventures grow and succeed by becoming an expert at these networking strategies.

The first networking tactics are for small businesses.

Networking is crucial for the survival and expansion of small businesses.
Effective networking strategies include the following:.

Identify Target Markets: Specify your ideal clients or customers and strategically network with people or groups who match your target profile.

Utilize Local Networks: To connect with regional business communities, take part in regional trade associations, business chambers, and community events.

Present Your Expertise: Establish yourself or your company as a subject-matter authority in your field by participating in webinars or speaking engagements.

Networking to Increase Your Clientele.

Whether you're in the B2B or B2C markets, networking is a powerful tool for growing your clientele.
Effective ways to expand your clientele include:.

Attend Industry-Specific Events: To network with potential customers, attend conferences, trade shows, and expos that are pertinent to your target market.

Leverage Online Platforms: Connect with prospective customers and promote your offerings by using social media and business networking sites.

Offer Value First: Before promoting your goods or services directly, concentrate on developing relationships and providing value.

3 Networking in groups to form business alliances.

Collaborative networking entails forming profitable alliances with other companies.
Utilize collaborative networking's potential by doing the following.

Find Businesses That Offer Complementary Products or Services: Look for companies that provide complementary products or services, and consider forming partnerships with them.

Explore strategic alliances, co-marketing initiatives, and joint ventures that can increase your reach.

Create Transparency: To ensure the longevity and success of your partnerships, create trust.

Whether you are a startup, small business, or established company, networking can be the key to business growth.
We'll explore advanced networking techniques and real-world examples in the upcoming chapters to help you further develop your networking skills. Prepare to use strategic networking to drive the growth and success of your company.

CHAPTER 9

PERSONAL GROWTH AND DEVELOPMENT THROUGH NETWORKING.

Nurturing Your Potential

Networking is not only for professional or business purposes, but it is also a powerful force for personal growth and development.
This chapter delves into leveraging networking for personal development.
We will explore networking for learning and skill growth, utilizing networking to find mentors and

role models, and establishing a strong support system through personal networking.
Integrating these strategies nurtures potential and enables continuous self-improvement.

Learning and Skill Development through Networking

Networking is beneficial for gaining knowledge and improving skills.
To utilize networking for learning and honing skills.

Find experts or knowledgeable groups to gain the insights or information you need.

Engage in Workshops and Seminars: Join workshops, seminars, or webinars led by industry experts in your field of interest.

Teach to learn: Share your expertise to empower others.

Connecting with Mentors and Role Models through Networking.

Mentors and role models are crucial for personal growth and development.
Networking aids in discovering these influential individuals.
Here\\\'s how:

Engage in Networking Events: Join events where you can meet experienced individuals open to mentoring.

Consult mentors respectfully, clearly requesting their guidance and support.

Gain inspiration from role models by studying their experiences and insights.

Establishing a Supportive Network through Personal Connections.

Networking is crucial for establishing a strong support system too.
To establish a personal network for support.

Build authentic relationships: Form deep connections with friends, acquaintances, and individuals who share your values.

Reach out to your support system for emotional
assistance in difficult situations.

Engage with your network to inspire, motivate, and
receive feedback for personal development.

Expanding one's personal growth and development
through networking is a life-long endeavor.
Focus on building meaningful relationships, not just
transactional interactions, to aid your journey of
self-improvement.
Upcoming chapters delve into advanced networking
techniques and real-life anecdotes showcasing
personal networking's significant influence on
individuals.
Get ready to explore personal growth and self-
discovery by leveraging the potential of networking.

CHAPTER 10

NAVIGATING NETWORKING OBSTACLES AND SETBACKS.

Developing resilience when faced with challenges

Networking is a rollercoaster ride.
In this chapter, we address potential obstacles and provide solutions to overcome them.
We'll cover ways to handle rejection and disappointment, recover from networking failures, and turn networking challenges into opportunities. Developing resilience helps you smoothly navigate your networking journey.

"Coping with Rejecti

Don't let rejection and disappointment hinder your
networking progress.
Here\\\'s how to cope:

Remember that rejection does not define your value,
often being influenced by timing or circumstances.

Seek feedback to improve.

Persist despite rejection in networking.
Continue exploring and pursuing fresh prospects.

Recovering from Networking Setbacks

Networking failures are stepping stones to success. To recover from networking failures:

Assess and ponder: Critique failures and pinpoint opportunities for growth.

Utilize Your Network: Contact your network for assistance, guidance, and potential prospects.

Stay Positive: Having a optimistic mindset aids in overcoming obstacles and continuing progress.

Overcoming Networking Challenges through Opportunities

Proper mindset can transform networking challenges.
Convert them into opportunities like this:

Flexibility is key—be open to adjusting your networking strategy when challenges arise.

Turn setbacks into opportunities for resilience and growth.

Get feedback: Connect with your network for fresh insights and different outlooks on your challenges.

Obstacles on your networking journey are actually redirecting paths, not barriers.

They can result in unforeseen opportunities, individual development, and improved abilities.

In the upcoming chapters, we'll examine advanced networking strategies, such as managing sensitive situations and using setbacks to spur personal development.

Get ready to become stronger and more resilient in networking.

CONCLUSION

UTILIZING THE POTENTIAL OF NETWORKING

Your Journey Begins

Reflect on the immense potential in your hands as we conclude this networking journey.
Networking builds connections and your future.
Reach your dreams, accomplish goals, and navigate life's maze with a supportive network.

You\\\'ve delved into networking extensively, covering its psychology and strategies for personal and professional growth.

You now know how to utilize your connections for career growth, business expansion, and personal progress.

You've learned to conquer obstacles and emerge stronger and tougher.

It's time to begin your networking journey, equipped with knowledge, determination, and the belief in the power of your network.

Networking is an ongoing, transformative process, not just a means to an end.

Your network mirrors your journey, an interwoven tapestry of connections and nurtured relationships.

Networking is no longer a choice, but a requirement in our interconnected society.

It's a bridge to unforeseen mentors, partners, friends, and opportunities.

Every encounter, conversation, and connection on this journey can shape your future.